SELECTED POEMS

D1428233

From the same publishers

Samuel Beckett

Novels

Dream of Fair to Middling Women (1932)
Murphy (1938)
Watt (1945)
First Love (1945)
Mercier and Camier (1946)
Molloy (1951)*
Malone Dies (1951)*

The Unnamable (1953) *
How It Is (1961)
Company (1980)**
Ill Seen Ill Said (1981)**
Worstward Ho (1983)**
* published together as the Trilogy
** published together as Nohow On

Short Prose

More Pricks than Kicks (1934)
Collected Short Prose (in preparation)
Beckett Shorts (see below)

Poetry

Collected Poems (1930-1978)
Anthology of Mexican Poetry
(translations)

Criticism

Proust & Three Dialogues with Georges Duthuit (1931,1949)
Disjecta (1929-1967)

Beckett Shorts (A collection of 12 short volumes to commemorate the writer's death in 1989)

1. Texts for Nothing (1947-52)
2. Dramatic Works and Dialogues (1938-67)
3. All Strange Away (1963)
4. Worstward Ho (1983)
5. Six Residua (1957-72)
6. For to End Yet Again (1960-75)

7. The Old Tune (1962)
8. First Love (1945)
9. As the Story Was Told
10. Three Novellas (1945-6)
11. Stirrings Still (1986-9)
12. Selected Poems (1930-85)

SELECTED POEMS

Samuel Beckett

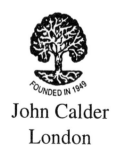

John Calder
London

This edition first published 1999 as a collection in Great Britain
by John Calder Publishers
London

All of these poems except *Go Where Never Before* and *Brief
Dream* were published previously in *Poems in English, Collected
Poems in English and French and Collected Poems 1930-1978*
© 1930, 1932, 1934, 1935, 1938, 1959, 1961, 1962, 1975, 1976,
1977, 1984, 1986, 1999. The French Poems were previously pub-
lished in France by Editions de Minuit, Paris, 1968.
Song first published in *Words and Music* by Faber and Faber 1962.
Tailpiece first published by Olympia Press 1953.

ISBN 0 7145 43055 Paperback

British Library Cataloguing in Publication Data
A catalogue record for this title is available from the British
Library

Printed by Webcom, Canada

CONTENTS

Whoroscope

What's that?
An egg?
By the brothers Boot it stinks fresh.
Give it to Gillot.

Galileo how are you
and his consecutive thirds!
The vile old Copernican lead-swinging son of a sutler!
We're moving he said we're off— Porca Madonna!
the way a boatswain would be, or a sack-of-potatoey
                             charging Pretender.
That's not moving, that's *moving*.   10

What's that?
A little green fry or a mushroomy one?
Two lashed ovaries with prostisciutto?
How long did she womb it, the feathery one?
Three days and four nights?
Give it to Gillot.

Faulhaber, Beeckman and Peter the Red,
come now in the cloudy avalanche or Gassendi's sun-red
                               crystally cloud
and I'll pebble you all your hen-and-a-half ones
or I'll pebble a lens under the quilt in the midst of day.   20

To think he was my own brother, Peter the Bruiser,
and not a syllogism out of him
no more than if Pa were still in it.
Hey! pass over those coppers,
sweet millèd sweat of my burning liver!
Them were the days I sat in the hot-cupboard throwing
                                    Jesuits out of the skylight.

Who's that? Hals?
Let him wait.

My squinty doaty!
I hid and you sook.   30
And Francine my precious fruit of a house-and-parlour
                                            foetus!
What an exfoliation!
Her little grey flayed epidermis and scarlet tonsils!
My one child
scourged by a fever to stagnant murky blood—
blood!
Oh Harvey belovèd
how shall the red and white, the many in the few,
(dear bloodswirling Harvey)
eddy through that cracked beater?   40
And the fourth Henry came to the crypt of the arrow.

What's that?
How long?
Sit on it.

A wind of evil flung my despair of ease
against the sharp spires of the one
lady:
not once or twice but . . . .
(Kip of Christ hatch it!)
in one sun's drowning   50
(Jesuitasters please copy).
So on with the silk hose over the knitted, and the morbid
                                                                leather—
what am I saying! the gentle canvas—
and away to Ancona on the bright Adriatic,
and farewell for a space to the yellow key of the
                                                                Rosicrucians.
They don't know what the master of them that do did,
that the nose is touched by the kiss of all foul and sweet air,
and the drums, and the throne of the faecal inlet,
and the eyes by its zig-zags.
So we drink Him and eat Him   60
and the watery Beaune and the stale cubes of Hovis
because He can jig
as near or as far from His Jigging Self
and as sad or lively as the chalice or the tray asks.
How's that, Antonio?

In the name of Bacon will you chicken me up that egg.
Shall I swallow cave-phantoms?

Anna Maria!
She reads Moses and says her love is crucified.
Leider! Leider! she bloomed and withered,   70
a pale abusive parakeet in a mainstreet window.

9

No I believe every word of it I assure you.
Fallor, ergo sum!
The coy old frôleur!
He tolle'd and legge'd
and he buttoned on his redemptorist waistcoat.
No matter, let it pass.
I'm a bold boy I know
so I'm not my son
(even if I were a concierge)   80
nor Joachim my father's
but the chip of a perfect block that's neither old nor new,
the lonely petal of a great high bright rose.

Are you ripe at last,
my slim pale double-breasted turd?
How rich she smells,
this abortion of a fledgling!
I will eat it with a fish fork.
White and yolk and feathers.
Then I will rise and move moving   90
toward Rahab of the snows,
the murdering matinal pope-confessed amazon,
Christina the ripper.
Oh Weulles spare the blood of a Frank
who has climbed the bitter steps,
(René du Perron . . . !)
and grant me my second
starless inscrutable hour.

1930

NOTES

René Descartes, Seigneur du Perron, liked his omelette made of eggs hatched from eight to ten days; shorter or longer under the hen and the result, he says, is disgusting.

He kept his own birthday to himself so that no astrologer could cast his nativity.

The shuttle of a ripening egg combs the warp of his days.

P. 1, l.   3   In 1640 the brothers Boot refuted Aristotle in Dublin.

4   Descartes passed on the easier problems in analytical geometry to his valet Gillot.

5–10   Refer to his comtempt for Galileo Jr., (whom he confused with the more musical Galileo Sr.), and to his expedient sophistry concerning the movement of the earth.

17   He solved problems submitted by these mathematicians.

P. 2, l. 21–26   The attempt at swindling on the part of his elder brother Pierre de la Bretaillière—The money he received as a soldier.

27   Franz Hals.

29–30   As a child he played with a little cross-eyed girl.

31–35   His daughter died of scarlet fever at the age of six.

37–40   Honoured Harvey for his discovery of the circulation of the blood, but would not admit that he had explained the motion of the heart.

41   The heart of Henri IV was received at the Jesuit college of La Flèche while Descartes was still a student there.

P. 3, l. 45–53   His visions and pilgrimage to Loretto.

56–65   His Eucharistic sophistry, in reply to the Jansenist Antoine Arnauld, who challenged him to reconcile his doctrine of matter with the doctrine of transubstantiation.

FROM ECHO'S BONES

The Vulture

dragging his hunger through the sky
of my skull shell of sky and earth

stooping to the prone who must
soon take up their life and walk

mocked by a tissue that may not serve
till hunger earth and sky be offal

Alba

before morning you shall be here
and Dante and the Logos and all strata and mysteries
and the branded moon
beyond the white plane of music
that you shall establish here before morning

>   grave suave singing silk
>   stoop to the black firmament of areca
>   rain on the bamboos flower of smoke alley of willows·

who though you stoop with fingers of compassion
to endorse the dust
shall not add to your bounty
whose beauty shall be a sheet before me
a statement of itself drawn across the tempest of emblems
so that there is no sun and no unveiling
and no host
only I and then the sheet
and bulk dead

Serena II

this clonic earth

see-saw she is blurred in sleep
she is fat half dead the rest is free-wheeling
part the black shag the pelt
is ashen woad
snarl and howl in the wood wake all the birds
hound the harlots out of the ferns
this damfool twilight threshing in the brake
bleating to be bloodied
this crapulent hush
tear its heart out

in her dreams she trembles again
way back in the dark old days panting
in the claws of the Pins in the stress of her hour
the bag writhes she thinks she is dying
the light fails it is time to lie down
Clew Bay vat of xanthic flowers
Croagh Patrick waned Hindu to spite a pilgrim
she is ready she has lain down above all the islands of glory
straining now this Sabbath evening of garlands
with a yo-heave-ho of able-bodied swans
out from the doomed land their reefs of tresses
in a hag she drops her young
the whales in Blacksod Bay are dancing

the asphodels come running the flags after
she thinks she is dying she is ashamed

she took me up on to a watershed
whence like the rubrics of a childhood
behold Meath shining through a chink in the hills
posses of larches there is no going back on
a rout of tracks and streams fleeing to the sea
kindergartens of steeples and then the harbour
like a woman making to cover her breasts
and left me

with whatever trust of panic we went out
with so much shall we return
there shall be no loss of panic between a man and his dog
bitch though he be

sodden packet of Churchman
muzzling the cairn
it is worse than dream
the light randy slut can't be easy
this clonic earth
all these phantoms shuddering out of focus
it is useless to close the eyes
all the chords of the earth broken like a woman pianist's
the toads abroad again on their rounds
sidling up to their snares
the fairy-tales of Meath ended
so say your prayers now and go to bed
your prayers before the lamps start to sing behind the larches
here at these knees of stone
then to bye-bye on the bones

Malacoda

thrice he came
the undertaker's man
impassible behind his scutal bowler
to measure
is he not paid to measure
this incorruptible in the vestibule
this malebranca knee-deep in the lilies
Malacoda knee-deep in the lilies
Malacoda for all the expert awe
that felts his perineum mutes his signal
sighing up through the heavy air
must it be it must be it must be
find the weeds engage them in the garden
hear she may see she need not

to coffin
with assistant ungulata
find the weeds engage their attention
hear she must see she need not

to cover
to be sure cover cover all over
your targe allow me hold your sulphur
divine dogday glass set fair
stay Scarmilion stay stay
lay this Huysum on the box
mind the imago it is he
hear she must see she must
all aboard all souls
half-mast aye aye

nay

Echo's Bones

asylum under my tread all this day
their muffled revels as the flesh falls
breaking without fear or favour wind
the gantelope of sense and nonsense run
taken by the maggots for what they are

1935

Cascando

1

why not merely the despaired of
occasion of
wordshed

is it not better abort than be barren

the hours after you are gone are so leaden
they will always start dragging too soon
the grapples clawing blindly the bed of want
bringing up the bones the old loves
sockets filled once with eyes like yours
all always is it better too soon than never
the black want splashing their faces
saying again nine days never floated the loved
nor nine months
nor nine lives

2
saying again
if you do not teach me I shall not learn
saying again there is a last
even of last times
last times of begging
last times of loving
of knowing not knowing pretending
a last even of last times of saying
if you do not love me I shall not be loved
if I do not love you I shall not love

the churn of stale words in the heart again
love love love thud of the old plunger
pestling the unalterable
whey of words

terrified again
of not loving
of loving and not you
of being loved and not by you
of knowing not knowing pretending
pretending

I and all the others that will love you
if they love you

3
unless they love you

1936

Roundelay

on all that strand
at end of day
steps sole sound
long sole sound
until unbidden stay
then no sound
on all that strand
long no sound
until unbidden go
steps sole sound
long sole sound
on all that strand
at end of day

1976

Song

Age is when to a man
Huddled o'er the ingle
Shivering for the hag
To put the pan in the bed
And bring the toddy
She comes in the ashes
Who loved could not be won
Or won not loved
Or some other trouble
Comes in the ashes
Like in that old light
The face in the ashes
That old starlight
On the earth again.

1962

Dieppe

again the last ebb
the dead shingle
the turning then the steps
towards the lights of old

my way is in the sand flowing
between the shingle and the dune
the summer rain rains on my life
on me my life harrying fleeing
to its beginning to its end

my peace is there in the receding mist
when I may cease from treading these long shifting
                                    thresholds
and live the space of a door
that opens and shuts

what would I do without this world faceless incurious
where to be lasts but an instant where every instant
spills in the void the ignorance of having been
without this wave where in the end
body and shadow together are engulfed
what would I do without this silence where the murmurs die
the pantings the frenzies towards succour towards love
without this sky that soars
above its ballast dust

what would I do what I did yesterday and the day before
peering out of my deadlight looking for another
wandering like me eddying far from all the living
in a convulsive space
among the voices voiceless
that throng my hiddenness

I would like my love to die
and the rain to be raining on the graveyard
and on me walking the streets
mourning her who thought she loved me

Something there

something there
where
out there
out where
outside
what
the head what else
something there somewhere outside
the head

at the faint sound so brief
it is gone and the whole globe
not yet bare
the eye
opens wide
wide
till in the end
nothing more
shutters it again

so the odd time
out there
somewhere out there
like as if
as if
something
not life
necessarily

1974

Go where never before
No sooner there than there always
No matter where never before
No sooner there than there always

for James Knowlson

Brief Dream

go end there
one fine day
where never till then
till as much as to say
no matter where
no matter when

Tailpiece

who may tell the tale
of the old man?
weigh absence in a scale?
mete want with a span?
the sum assess
of the world's woes?
nothingness
in words enclose?